A Close Friendship with God

Although my youth was filled with religion, God was missing. My life in those days revolved around the parish: Sunday Mass, parochial school, First Holy Communion, sports teams, service as an altar boy, confirmation, teen club, and, finally, a large Catholic wedding. It was not until after graduation from college that I came to know God in a personal sense. Through reading the New Testament, I found God's way of salvation and a Savior who promised, "I have come that they may have life, and have it to the full" (John 10:10).

Although no longer a Catholic, my heart remains with the Catholic people. I owe much to them, especially my family and the priests and nuns who so lovingly cared for me. It is for this reason that I have written this booklet. I am concerned that others are as I was. They have been baptized and go to Mass, yet deep within they feel that God is a stranger.

How about you? Do you know Him? Is He the center of your life? *What Every Catholic Should Ask* raises important questions that every Catholic should consider. Supplying answers from the Sacred Scriptures, it explains how you can have a close friendship with God. It also shows how you can be certain of living with Him in heaven forever.

What Every
CATHOLIC
SHOULD ASK

This is a gift from
Goldings Church
Englands Lane, Loughton
079314 12380
020 8590 1651
Pastor Jeremy Sandy
Sunday Services 11.am / 6.30pm
With British Sign Language Interpreting

James G. McCarthy

HARVEST HOUSE PUBLISHERS
Eugene, Oregon 97402

Cover by Terry Dugan Design, Minneapolis, Minnesota

Those seeking documentation for the statements made about Roman Catholicism in this book should refer to *The Gospel According to Rome* (Harvest House Publishers, 1995) by the same author. Keyed to the *Catechism of the Catholic Church,* it contains over 500 footnotes and 1000 cross references to official Catholic sources.

Correspondence or requests for additional information on this topic can be sent to Good News for Catholics, PO Box 595, Cupertino, CA 95015, USA.

Other Books by
James G. McCarthy

The Gospel According to Rome

What You Need to Know About Roman Catholicism
Quick Reference Guide

WHAT EVERY CATHOLIC SHOULD ASK
Copyright © 1999 by James G. McCarthy
Published by Harvest House Publishers
Eugene, Oregon 97402

Library of Congress Cataloging-in-Publication Data
ISBN 0-7369-0001-2

Printed in the United States of America.

02   03   04   05   06   07   /LC/   10   9   8   7   6   5   4

Can Anyone Know?

I write these things to you who believe in the name of the Son of God so that you may know that you have eternal life.

1 JOHN 5:13

W hen Jane, a Catholic schoolteacher, was first shown the above verse she misread it four times. Each time she left out three words. She read: "I write these things to you who believe in the name of the Son of God so that you may have eternal life." The verse actually ends: "so that you may *know that you* have eternal life."

From childhood Jane had been taught that no one knows until death whether he or she is going to heaven. She had been told that anyone might commit a mortal sin, die in a state of sin, and end up in hell. That is why Jane kept misreading the verse. She read it the way she thought it should be read. Only after someone pointed out her error did she realize what she was doing. "I didn't think anyone could *know* they were going to heaven," Jane explained.

That's how many people think. But the Bible teaches the opposite. It says that you can be positive that you are going to heaven. For example, it says that "everyone who calls on the name of the Lord will be saved" (Romans 10:13). In the same chapter is the promise: "Anyone who trusts in him will never be put to shame" (Romans 10:11).

Jesus also taught: "I tell you the truth, whoever hears my word and believes him who sent me has eternal life and will not be condemned; he has crossed over from death to life" (John 5:24). Note that Jesus says that the one who *believes in Him has eternal life.* Heaven can be your present possession. God is willing to reserve a place for you in heaven right now.

Consider what this means. You can have confidence that upon death you will go straight to heaven. You don't even have to show up on that terrible day when God will judge the sins of others. You can be like the thief on the cross to whom Jesus promised, "I tell you the truth, today you will be with me in paradise" (Luke 23:43).

Before eternal life can be yours, however, you must understand how sin has separated you from God.

How Does God See Me?

Search me, O God, and know my heart;
test me and know my anxious thoughts.
See if there is any offensive way in me,
and lead me in the way everlasting.

PSALM 139:23,24

We all need God to search our hearts and show us what we are really like. Left to ourselves, we tend to underestimate our sinfulness. We compare ourselves with those around us, judge ourselves to be average or above, and figure things can't be that bad. We know that we have sinned, but excuse ourselves, reasoning "I'm only human."

Then along comes someone with what seems like a suitable remedy. "Practice your religion," this person tells us, "and everything will be fine. Believe in God, go to church, and receive the sacraments. Live a decent life in obedience to the Ten Commandments, and try to be kind to everyone. If you do these things," he assures us, "you should go to heaven."

Yet, what if our sin is more serious than we thought? What if our best isn't good enough? What if what we are doing won't get us to heaven? Using Scripture, let's look at what God says about sin. Though you may find the topic unpleasant, please don't skip this section. Unless you understand your sin problem, and take it to heart, you cannot understand God's solution for it.

Also, as you read, don't make excuses, minimize, blame others, or let religious pride blind you to your sins. Honestly own up to your sin. Only then will you be able to understand how to get rid of your guilt.

You will need God's help for the courage to do this, so stop and talk to God in prayer. Ask Him to allow you to see yourself as He sees you. Tell Him that you want to know the full extent of your sin. In doing so, you will be preparing your heart to receive God's promise of eternal life.

What Went Wrong?

The LORD God commanded the man, "You are free to eat from any tree in the garden; but you must not eat from the tree of the knowledge of good and evil, for when you eat of it you will surely die."

GENESIS 2:16,17

God intended for Adam and Eve to enjoy the Garden of Eden with Him forever. They, however, chose to rebel against Him, disobeying His direct command. This offended God, broke the close friendship Adam and Eve had enjoyed with Him, and, as He had warned, brought death into the world.

Adam's sin, which the Catholic Church calls *original sin,* passed to his descendants. With it came "condemnation for all men" (Romans 5:18). Consequently, you and I were born under the curse of sin. We all have sinful hearts, are destined to die, and are headed for hell. The evidence that we are born sinners is undeniable. No one has to teach us how to lie, to hate, to commit sexual immorality, to abuse alcohol or drugs, to cheat, to steal. These things come to us naturally.

We sin in our thoughts, words, and actions. The Penitential Rite recited during Mass expresses this: "I confess to almighty God, and to you, my brothers and sisters, that I have sinned through my own fault in my thoughts and in my words, in what I have done, and in what I have failed to do." The Bible says that our hearts are deceitful above all things (Jeremiah 17:9). Our thoughts, as God sees them, are continually toward evil (Genesis 6:5). There is an element of selfishness, pride, anger, lust, greed, or impurity in almost everything we do.

We can see the consequences of human sin all around us. Just turn on the evening news or read the newspaper. Sin has infected our lives and polluted our planet with injustice, suffering, hatred, and bloodshed. What God created in purity and splendor has become filthy and corrupt under our management.

We are unfit to live with God in His holiness in heaven. Scripture says that "nothing impure will ever enter it, nor will anyone who does what is shameful or deceitful" (Revelation 21:27). That leaves us out. If God let us in the way we are, heaven would soon be as contaminated with evil as we have made this earth.

Death is our destiny because it is the penalty for sin. It is the reason we all eventually die, despite the best efforts of modern medicine. But the curse of sin is not just physical death (the separation of our souls from our bodies); it is also spiritual death (the separation of our spirit from God). Sin keeps us from God. It is the reason why He seems so distant, so unlike us. We can sense our alienation from Him.

If we die with the guilt of sin still upon us, God will condemn us on the day of judgment. We will experience His wrath, entering what the Bible calls "the second death" (Revelation 20:14) or "hell" (Matthew 10:28). There we will spend eternity separated from Him forever.

Yet God gives us hope. He has good news of salvation for us.

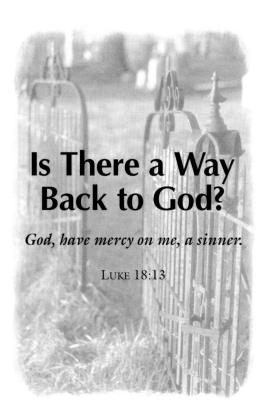

Is There a Way Back to God?

God, have mercy on me, a sinner.

LUKE 18:13

God has a solution for our sin that can lift the death penalty from our souls and change us, making us fit for heaven. His solution can restore us to a close friendship with Him. But before it can be ours, God requires that we confess our guilt before Him. This admission means more than just agreeing that everyone sins. Each of us must confess, "Lord, *I* am a sinner."

Simply repeating the words or performing a ritual, such as the sacrament of confession, is not enough. At Mass, during the Communion Rite, for example, you say with the priest, "Lord, I am not worthy to receive You, but only say the word and I shall be healed." Those are good words, but do you really see yourself as an *unworthy* sinner?

Too many of us are like Mary, a Catholic woman I met as she came out of Mass. I asked her what answer she would give to God for her sins when she stood in the final judgment. Mary replied, "I'm not sure that what I've done in the past could ever be reconciled. But there's nothing horrible either. I'm not a murderer or anything like that."

That is how the religious people of Jesus' day thought about their sins. They knew they had sinned, but they didn't see themselves as bad people. They weren't adulterers and murderers. There wasn't anything "horrible" in their lives, no serious sins—or so they thought.

Jesus told them otherwise. He said that if a man so much as looks at a woman lustfully, he "has already committed adultery with her in his heart" (Matthew 5:28). He said that anyone who angrily calls another person a fool would be "in danger of the fire of hell" (Matthew 5:22). The Bible says "there is no one righteous, not even one" (Romans 3:10), and "all have sinned and fall short of the glory of God" (Romans 3:23).

Just as in Jesus' day, we can deceive ourselves into thinking we are good people because we are "religious." All too easily we start acting like the Pharisee in the parable who went up to the temple and prayed, "God, I thank you that I am not like other men— robbers, evildoers, adulterers—or even like this tax collector" (Luke 18:11). The Pharisee was referring to a "real" sinner standing next to him. This other man, a Jew who had betrayed his people by working as a tax collector for the Romans, was broken- hearted over his sins. Ashamed before God, he was unwilling even to look up to heaven. He kept beating his breast, saying, "God, have mercy on me, a sinner" (Luke 18:13).

Jesus said of the tax collector, "I tell you that this man, rather than the other, went home justified before God. For everyone who exalts himself will be humbled, and he who humbles himself will be exalted" (Luke 18:14).

What about you? Are you a guilty sinner? Will you humble yourself before God and say from your heart, "Lord, be merciful to me, a sinner"?

If so, God is ready to help you.

God's Will or Mine?

"The time has come," he said. "The kingdom of God is near. Repent and believe the good news!"

MARK 1:15

The good news Jesus announced to the world is God's solution to our sin. And the solution is available to all who would repent and believe.

Repentance comes first. It is a change of mind about self and God that prepares your heart to receive God's salvation. It begins with listening to your conscience, that small voice within you. God gave it to you to help you know right from wrong. It is there to bother you when you offend God, producing a sense of shame, guilt, and remorse. But your conscience usually speaks in a whisper. To hear it, you must be willing to listen.

The next step in repentance is *confessing* your sin. It is saying, "Lord, I agree with You that I have done wrong. I have sinned against You and those around me. I make no excuses for my sins."

Finally, repentance must include *a change of mind* about how you are going to live. It is a desire *to turn from sin* to God, a submitting of yourself to His authority. Repentance is saying, "Lord, I want a new life, the kind of life that pleases You. I want to do what You want me to do, if You will make me able." One man described his decision to repent this way: "For the first time, I decided to put God's will before my own."

Repentance is not a resolution to reform your life to earn God's favor. You sin because by nature you are a sinner. That is something you cannot change. Consequently, you will never find acceptance with God by trying to clean up your life and do better. Neither does repentance involve a vow to do penance. You can't make up for your sins by going to Mass, praying the Rosary, obtaining indulgences, abstaining from certain foods, doing good deeds, offering up your sufferings, or even entering the religious life. The penalty for sin is death. Nothing short of that can pay for sin.

God does not ask you to reform your life or to do penance. Instead, He calls you to repent—

- Ask the Holy Spirit to show you your sin. Tell Him you want to experience the guilt that is rightfully yours for having offended God.

- Take inventory of your life. Ask yourself if there is any sin in your life that you're not willing to give up.

- If you are ready to turn from your sins, confess them to God. Express to Him your sorrow for what you have done. Mention by name those sins for which you are especially ashamed.

- Tell God that from now on you want to live life His way, if He will give you the ability. Acknowledge before God that you cannot change yourself or make up for your sins.

- Finally, ask God to show you His solution for your sin. Do this in faith, believing Jesus' promise to help anyone who is willing to do God's will (John 7:17).

The next pages will explain from the Scriptures how you can have your sins forgiven, enter into a true friendship with God, and be certain you are going to heaven.

14

Why Did Jesus Come?

*"The virgin will be with child and
will give birth to a son, and they
will call him Immanuel"—which
means, "God with us."*

A s most people are aware, the Christian Scriptures teach
that there is only one true God. He exists in three persons—the
Father, the Son, and the Holy Spirit. The Father is God. The Son
is God. The Holy Spirit is God. Yet God is one.

Jesus, the Son of God, was born of the Virgin Mary and
became a man. He did this without giving up His nature as God.
For this reason, Jesus is true God and true man, the God-man.
Why did Jesus take on human nature? Answer that question cor-
rectly, and you will have the solution to your sin problem.

Some say Jesus became a man to show us how to live. "Do as He did," they promise, "and you'll make it to heaven." The Bible agrees, at least in part, telling us that we ought to "walk as Jesus did" (1 John 2:6). The problem, of course, is *who can do that?* Jesus, having no earthly father, was born without a sin nature. You and I, on the other hand, as children of Adam, are born sinners. We are unable to get to heaven by living like Jesus.

Another reason some people give for Jesus' becoming a man is that "He came to show us the love of God." That is also true. In Christ we see that God is love, and that He loves us. But understanding this does not get us to heaven. To the contrary, when we compare God's love to our own, we see how unloving and selfish we are—how unfit we are for heaven.

"Jesus came to be a sacrifice," others say. When asked why, these same people often just shrug their shoulders. "It has something to do with the Old Testament," is all they can offer.

Each of these answers is partially correct. None of them, however, explains *why* the Son of God took on human nature and how that made it possible for us to be reconciled to God and to go to heaven.

Why Did Jesus Die?

For even the Son of Man
did not come to be served,
but to serve, and to give
his life as a ransom for many.

MARK 10:45

The above verse tells us the main reason Jesus became a man. It was so He could serve humankind by giving His life for us. Think about it; it makes sense.

God warned Adam that the punishment for sin was death. That is also true for us. The New Testament says "the wages of sin is death" (Romans 6:23). What we earn for our sin is the death penalty. And not even God can release us from this sentence without its being paid. He has made a judgment against us, and He cannot disregard His decision. He cannot ignore our sin if He is to remain fair, just, and true to His word.

Nevertheless, God wants to forgive us. He loves us and desires to save us from hell. Is there a way He can spare us and yet remain just? There is a solution, but only one—an amazing one. Jesus, the Son of God, volunteered to come to earth "to give his life as a ransom for many" (Mark 10:45). That is what He did on the cross. He gave *His* life as the payment for our sins. *He died in our place.*

The apostle Peter explains it this way: "Christ died for sins once for all, the righteous for the unrighteous, to bring you to God" (1 Peter 3:18). Jesus, *the righteous one,* died on behalf of you and me, *the unrighteous ones.* He offered this payment *once for all.* His perfect life given at the cross was enough to pay for *all* our sins. No further payment is necessary. We have been redeemed by the "precious blood of Christ" (1 Peter 1:19).

Following Christ's crucifixion, His disciples buried Him in a tomb. On the third day, God raised Jesus from the dead. In this way the Father showed that He accepted Christ's offering for our sins (Romans 4:25). Following His resurrection, Jesus appeared many times to His disciples, including a group of more than 500 people (1 Corinthians 15:6). He "gave many convincing proofs that he was alive" (Acts 1:3), and He spoke to them of His coming kingdom. After 40 days He ascended into heaven, having told His followers that He was going to prepare a place for them. Jesus promised, "I will come back and take you to be with me" (John 14:3).

If the meaning and importance of Christ's death, resurrection, and promise to return is not clear to you, ask God to help you understand.

What Is God Offering?

For it is by grace you have been saved, through faith—and this not from yourselves, it is the gift of God—not by works, so that no one can boast.

EPHESIANS 2:8,9

$\mathcal{S}$ince Jesus' death on the cross was enough to pay for all sin, God is now able to make you a wonderful offer. He wants to forgive your *every* sin—past, present, and future—and to stamp the record of your sins *paid in full.* He wants to break the power that sin has over you, make you a new creation, and change you into the likeness of Christ. God is ready to bring you into His family and have you live with Him in heaven forever.

God is willing to do all this for you "by grace." Acting out of His love, generosity, and kindness, He wants to bless you beyond description. This great salvation is "the gift of God." It costs you nothing because Christ has already paid the awful price. You do not have to earn it; it is not by works. What could you do to earn forgiveness and eternal life in heaven anyway?

"I think I'll make it to heaven," a Catholic woman told me as we stood in front of her parish church, "by going to church, living a good life, and keeping the Ten Commandments. I think I have a pretty good chance."

That poor woman hasn't any chance at all. The Bible says that no one will get to heaven by keeping the Ten Commandments. That is not their purpose. God gave them to us to show us how far short we fall of His perfect standard. "Through the law we become conscious of sin" (Romans 3:20). The law helps us see that we need a Savior, that we need Jesus.

"I think the good in my life will outweigh the bad," another Catholic told me outside the same church. That man hasn't a chance either. All the good works in the world can't make up for one sin. Neither can suffering for a time either here on earth or later in a place like purgatory, as some people propose. The penalty for sin is death, eternal separation from God.

You can't work your way to heaven. That's a hopeless endeavor. Instead, praise God that He sent His Son to die for you! Thank Him that He is willing to forgive your sins and give you eternal life as a gift.

What Must I Do?

"Sirs, what must I do to be saved?"
They replied, "Believe in the Lord
Jesus, and you will be saved—you
and your household."

ACTS 16:30,31

What must we do to receive God's gift of salvation? "Believe in the Lord Jesus, and you will be saved." Maybe you are thinking, *What's new about that? I've always believed in Jesus.* You probably accept the basic historic truths about Christ. And you may have recited the Apostle's Creed at Mass more than a thousand times.

Believing in Jesus for salvation, however, means more than agreeing with certain facts about Him. It also means to rely upon Him to make you right with God. It is to place your faith in Christ as the One who died in your place, taking your punishment for you. It is to trust Him, and Him alone, to rescue you from the coming wrath. God's Word says that salvation is in Jesus and "no one else, for there is no other name under heaven given to men by which we must be saved" (Acts 4:12).

If you have never trusted Jesus to save you from the punishment of sin, you can receive Him as your Savior now:

- Salvation starts with repentance. If you have not done so already, humble yourself before God, admitting your sin and guilt. Express your desire to do His will, trusting Him to give you the ability to do what is right.

- Next, place your trust in the Lord Jesus to save you. Tell God you are relying on Christ's death on the cross as the complete payment for your sins.

- State before God that you are not going to depend upon anyone or anything else for your salvation—not yourself, your priest, Mary, the saints, the Church, your baptism, your participation in the other sacraments, your attempts to obey the Ten Commandments—not even your good works. Tell God you have decided to trust Jesus, and Jesus alone, for your salvation.

- Thank God for His free offer of forgiveness and eternal life. Acknowledge that you do not deserve such generous treatment, but humbly accept it as a gift from God.

You can do this today, speaking to God in prayer, in your own words. Once you do so, tell your family and friends of your decision to repent and trust Jesus to save you. Encourage them to do the same. The Bible says that God's offer of salvation is for "you and your household" (Acts 16:31).

What Happened to the Good News?

He said to them: "You have a fine way of setting aside the commands of God in order to observe your own traditions!"

MARK 7:9

God gave the nation of Israel its religion at Mount Sinai, speaking to the Israelites through Moses. By the time Jesus came, 1400 years later, they had departed from the truth. They had set aside the written record of God's instructions, the Old Testament Scriptures, in order to follow the traditions of their teachers and leaders. Jesus harshly rebuked them for this (see Mark 7:1-13).

Sadly, the Roman Catholic Church has made the same error. Following the traditions of men, it has departed from the true Christian faith by setting aside God's Word. The Church no longer teaches salvation by grace alone through faith alone because of Christ alone, as found in Sacred Scripture. No longer does it proclaim Jesus' message, "Repent and believe the good news!" (Mark 1:15).

Today Rome teaches that heaven is a reward *earned* by performing good deeds with the help of God. To get to heaven you must obtain *sanctifying grace* in your soul and keep it there until death. To accomplish this, the Church says, you must do ten things:

- believe in God
- be baptized
- be a loyal member of the Catholic Church
- love God
- love your neighbor
- keep the Ten Commandments
- receive the sacraments, especially Holy Communion
- pray
- do good works
- die in a state of grace with no unconfessed mortal sins

Striving to get to heaven by doing those ten things *is not* the message of salvation brought by Christ and recorded by the Holy Spirit in the New Testament. There, God promises, "Believe in the Lord Jesus, and you will be saved" (Acts 16:31). Eternal life, according to the Bible, is not an earned reward but *the gift of God* (Romans 6:23).

God's Word or Man's Word?

Sanctify them by the truth; your word is truth.

JOHN 17:17

God used men to write the Bible. What they wrote, however, was not their own ideas. Peter says that the writers "were carried along by the Holy Spirit" (2 Peter 1:21). Scripture, therefore, is God's Word. It is inspired, "God-breathed" (2 Timothy 3:16).

As such, the Bible contains only truth. God has provided it "for teaching, rebuking, correcting and training in righteousness, so that the man of God may be thoroughly equipped for every good work" (2 Timothy 3:16,17). It is the perfect guide to the Christian faith.

The Catholic Church disagrees. It says that the Bible is not enough. One must also follow Tradition, the *unwritten* teachings that supposedly live within the Church, having been passed down for centuries. The Church says that Catholics must give Tradition the same honor they give Scripture.

In addition, the pope and bishops say that only *they* can determine the true meaning of Scripture and Tradition. Since they claim to be "the successors of the 12 apostles," their decisions are final. No one may question their teachings.

Christ and His apostles, by contrast, told the first Christians to "test everything" (1 Thessalonians 5:21). They taught their followers to use Scripture as the standard for judging the truthfulness of all teaching and to beware of "false apostles, deceitful workmen, masquerading as apostles of Christ" (2 Corinthians 11:13).

We have already seen how Tradition has changed the original message of salvation. Now let's look at how it has affected the Catholic view of Mass and Mary.

How Shall I Worship Christ?

He took bread, gave thanks and
broke it, and gave it to them, saying,
"This is my body given for you; do
this in remembrance of me."

<small>Luke 22:19</small>

At the Last Supper, Christ asked His followers to take bread and wine to remember Him. These were to serve as *symbols* of His body and blood. Such symbols would help Christians focus their worship on what Christ had done for them on the cross. In this way they would "proclaim the Lord's death until he comes" (1 Corinthians 11:26).

The Roman Catholic Church has changed this simple act into a mysterious ritual. No longer is the goal merely to *remember* Christ with bread and wine around a table. Now, following Tradition, the priest supposedly *sacrifices* Christ on an altar. This occurs during the Mass when the priest repeats Christ's words at the Last Supper. The Church claims that at that moment the bread and wine change into Jesus' actual body and blood. Those present are to adore them as divine. Elevating the bread and wine above the altar, the priest then re-presents Christ in His victimhood to the Father. The Church says this offering makes satisfaction for the sins of the living and the dead. It is a real sacrifice, the Church claims, the sacrifice of the cross.

This ritual has no biblical basis. Nowhere do we read in the Scriptures of the first Christians attempting to sacrifice Christ with bread and wine. The cross was a horrific event in which Jesus' enemies tortured Him to death. Why would Christians want to continue it?

Once was enough. As Jesus died on the cross, He said, "It is finished" (John 19:30). He "offered for all time one sacrifice for sins" (Hebrews 10:12). "There is no longer any sacrifice for sin" (Hebrews 10:18). Further, Christ is now glorified in heaven. He is not a victim to be offered in continual sacrifice. The Bible says that "since Christ was raised from the dead, he cannot die again; death no longer has mastery over him" (Romans 6:9). Nevertheless, the Roman Catholic Church says that the sacrifice of the cross must continually be renewed. This is necessary, it claims, to carry out the work of redemption. That is why Catholic priests perform the Sacrifice of the Mass some 120 million times each year.

Each of us must choose how we will worship Christ. Our understanding of salvation will affect this decision. If we hope to get to heaven through a lifelong process of sacraments, obedience, and good works, then we will probably feel the need for an ongoing sacrifice, such as the Mass. If, on the other hand, we are trusting Christ's death on the cross as the perfect and sufficient offering for our sins, we will want to celebrate His *finished* work. Our desire will be to worship with Christians who use bread and wine as symbols *to remember* Christ, not *to sacrifice* Him.

Who Is the Real Mary?

*The angel went to her and said,
"Greetings, you who are highly
favored! The Lord is with you."*

LUKE 1:28

The New Testament presents Mary as a dedicated servant of God. When the angel Gabriel told her that God had chosen her to bear the Christ-child, she humbly accepted. " 'I am the Lord's servant,' Mary answered. 'May it be to me as you have said' " (Luke 1:38).

The Scriptures mention Mary briefly in relation to several events in Jesus' life. At the wedding feast at Cana, when the wine ran out, Mary asked Jesus to help, instructing the servants, "Do whatever he tells you" (John 2:5). (Good advice for us all.) As

Jesus hung on the cross, Mary was standing nearby (John 19:25). After Christ's ascension, she returned with the disciples to the upper room. There she devoted herself to prayer (Acts 1:14).

The Bible says nothing about the remainder of Mary's life. Indeed, taken as a whole, it has little to say about her.

The Catholic Church, by contrast, has a great deal to say about Mary, often going far beyond the biblical record. For example, the Church says that Mary was born free of original sin. It calls this the "doctrine of the Immaculate Conception." In 1854, Pope Pius IX declared it dogma, an official teaching allegedly received from God. Though the Bible says that "all have sinned and fall short of the glory of God" (Romans 3:23), the Church says that Mary never sinned.

The Church also teaches that at the end of Mary's life God took her bodily into heaven. This is the "doctrine of the Assumption of Mary." Pope Pius XII declared it a dogma in 1950. The Bible makes no mention of God taking Mary into heaven.

The Church says that Mary sits enthroned in heaven as "Queen of Heaven and Earth." It instructs the faithful to praise her as "Virgin Most Powerful," "Mother of Mercy," "Seat of Wisdom," and "All-Holy." People are to direct their prayers to her as "Advocate," "Helper," "Mother of Grace" (through whom all blessings flow), and "Mediatrix" (the feminine form of *mediator).*

The Bible reserves such titles for God. It teaches that there is "one mediator between God and men, the man Christ Jesus" (1 Timothy 2:5). It tells Christians to bring their needs directly to their heavenly Father in Jesus' name (John 14:13,14). Nowhere in the Bible is there an example of anyone praying to Mary or to the saints.

Finally, the Church says that Mary is the "Refuge of Sinners." Catholics should surrender their souls at the hour of their death wholly to her care, according to the *Catechism of the Catholic Church.* By contrast, the Bible says that we should put our complete trust in Christ to save us (Romans 10:8-13).

Where Do I Go from Here?

Now the Bereans were of more noble character than the Thessalonians, for they received the message with great eagerness and examined the Scriptures every day to see if what Paul said was true.

Acts 17:11

After Christ's resurrection and ascension into heaven, His disciples went throughout the world preaching the good news of salvation. Most who heard their message rejected it, and some even became angry and hostile. But others listened and considered. Among these were the people of Berea. The Bible says they were "of more noble character." They were interested in what the apostle Paul had to say, but they also wanted to confirm for themselves that it was correct. Therefore, they "examined the Scriptures every day to see if what Paul said was true." When they were convinced that his teaching agreed with God's Word, they received Paul's message and trusted Christ to save them.

Each of us needs to do the same. Taking personal responsibility for our souls, we must search out the truth and respond to God accordingly. The guide below is designed to help you. Start with prayer, asking God to give you wisdom, then trust Him to lead you through His Word. You will not be disappointed.

Essential Teachings on Jesus, Salvation, and Grace

Jesus' invitation to a personal relationship with Him	**Matthew 11:25-30; John 10:1-18**
A record of Jesus' teaching and life written to explain how to receive eternal life through faith in Him	**Gospel of John**
The fullest explanation of salvation in the Bible	**Romans 1:16–5:21**
A warning against the error of trying to get to heaven though faith and good works	**Letter to the Galatians**
A history of the early church, recording the preaching of the apostles and how the first Christians practiced their faith	**Acts of the Apostles**
Paul's renunciation of dependence upon religious practices for salvation	**Philippians 3:1-11**
An explanation of how true, saving faith shows itself in good deeds	**James 2:14-26**
Two poetic descriptions of the crucifixion of Christ made by Jewish prophets hundreds of years before Jesus came to earth	**Psalm 22; Isaiah 53**
The Lord's request that Christians take bread and wine to remember Him	**Matthew 26:26-30; Mark 14:22-25; Luke 22:14-20; 1 Corinthians 11:17-34**
The superiority of Christ's once-for-all-time sacrifice	**Hebrews 9:1–10:18**
Every passage with reference to Mary in the New Testament	**Matthew 1:18–2:23; 12:46-50; 13:55,56; Mark 3:20-35; 6:3,4; Luke 1:26–2:51; 8:19-21; John 2:1-12; 6:42; 19:25-27; Acts 1:14; Galatians 4:4**